TEETH
of
HAVOC

TEETH
of
HAVOC

Poems of Apocalypse

---

by Sarah Soward

Published in the United States by Sarah Soward.
https://sarahsoward.com
Names: Soward, Sarah, author
Title: Teeth of Havoc, Poems of Apocalypse / Sarah Soward
Description: California : Sarah Soward, 2026.

ISBN 979-8-950190-00-1 (Paperback)
ISBN 979-8-950190-01-8 (ePub)
First Edition

Subjects:
POE023010 Poetry — Subjects & Themes; Death, Grief, Loss.
POE024000 Poetry — Women Authors.
POE023060 Poetry — Subjects & Themes; Political & Protest.

Cover art, cover and book design © 2026 Sarah Soward

Dedication

Hey there, Mr. Fox.
There'd be no Anymore without you.

Acknowledgments

Heartfelt thanks to Marco Castaneda and Jodie MacDonald for edits, insight, and general poetic critique.

Stubborn, pounding, and desolate thanks to the cacophonous, rancorous, and wily Ferrets who encouraged this sort of creative nonsense in me. The impact of each of you in my psyche could have obliterated dinosaurs. In lieu of fossils, oil fields, or flowers, have words. All of this is somehow both of your faults, my glorious dead friends.

Contents

Analog

Groove deep into
    my record player
Sing defiance
    to my face

You Didn't Save my Life Once

Smile
Count to three
Smile
Step back
Smile
A little further
        Please

Thalassa wrapped one hand inside
        my throat and grew

In one concussive movement she
        consumed me into the sea
Some part of it felt like home
        but that may have just been
                the hostility

The racket of my sister
        Wailing
Demanding comfort for the near-loss of…
        me…from the people still
                fishing
        for me

I am sand and brine
Seashells and broken glass

Lifted
        Pardoned
Heaved up from the salt
        Hosed down from the sea

It wasn't terror
        only drowning

Why is my sister still screaming
        Can she see the monsters at my back

Shhhh

(I heard the singing when it took you
      There was melody in your death
Sight unspoken
      Breathing broken)

The distance measured by footfalls and dog bites
      Is the laughter of your vice
(Once threatened
      Now deafened)

Reality is a sand castle made of crawling ants
      (Daffodils in a boxing match)
By chance
      They dance

The rope of your mind set free and lashed out
      Focused light through curved glass
Burn
      (Churn)

Images of ash and bone
      You're the irate side of stardust
        Ringing in my veins

In the Low

I doused myself
         in your ashes
Tasted cranberries on my lips

But that's a lie
I can't breathe in the dust of your death

The tape on your cardboard box is unbroken

They're waiting to divvy you up
         carry you home and wear you like a totem

Maybe they'll eat you
         Breathe you in
         Mix paint into a grim remembrance

You could have been anything

But that's a lie too

You were always going to end up
         dried out and sized down
         in a box

I miss the taste of cranberries

Resurrection is Hard
(Response to James Finn's "Am Dead")

I conspired to keep my clothing and my honor
I cut my hair and threw my story to the wind
To hurt myself, I kept the name that I found hateful
I refused to turn up simply dead

My dreams were big but too small for me
My nightmares, a crime report we all know
While terrors that I refuse to share
Paralyze me sleeping like the dead

Revenge and justice are not two sides nor two-sided
Running is the haven of my youth
All that fighting broke my body, nose to toe beds
My wits alone saved me from becoming dead

Hours and days mean little in my life math
The longitude of location does not suit
I learned my comfort was mere endurance
What I lived fed my shadows to the dead

Sometimes death was what nearly killed me
For that, I cast myself an artful copy
Planted in the earth with chaotic glory
To quell my longing for our beloved dead

I made paintings bigger than my horror
Placed to wear my trauma into dust
It didn't work because art is respected
While people like me have no value, even dead

I could not stay on the stage they cast me
The only sane response was to exit out the back

As I flew I flayed away what I remembered
Of the constricting skin designed to squeeze me dead

The palace of my mind sifts through forgiveness
Its residue a grime of deprecation
The graffiti of abuse and denigration
Fades each time I'm found there, presumed dead

Maybe I was right to pound the Earth
Maybe I'm not the poison in my head
It could be I'm just another person
Who rises up each time they're pronounced dead

Are Dead/All Dead

As many ways
        to live
As turtles can be
        stacked

Imagine pancakes and beer
Ice cream with vodka sauce
A profundity of kittens

As many ways
        to run
As there are pebbles
        on a path

Believe there are diamonds made of grass
Safety in numbers
A reasonable hour to start the day

As many days
        to live
As mass hallucination
        gives

Consider space travel
A critical mass of weather balloons
The set-ability of clocks

Drink the pancakes
        and eat the beer
All we are
        is here

It's Okay to Get to the Point

I'm not all that good at it
Getting to the point
The roundabout way is full of
  ideas and secrets

Birds meet, shriek, nest, and treat
Sometimes they even beat the
  wings off each other
You can't see that from the road

It can be softer on the off-way too
Feet are cushioned
  where rocks aren't strewn

Of course there's danger here
  More than birds and bee stings
The dark behind distractions
  Blink and wink

But those wolves seem worth
  the whispers
Speaking rhythms to the wind

Petal to the Flower

No big deal
    It's only identity

How big of a sense of Me
    Does one need?
Chrysanthemum
    or pansy?

The power's in the petal

Pluck one
    Not done
Pluck three
    Still me
At five
    Am I still alive?

This is a metaphor
    for
violence against women

It's the beat down of daily life
    Micro-aggressions
    Macro-murders
The between acts
    that somehow won't land most
Behind bars

Side note
    It's only deflowering
    If it's against one's will
Otherwise

You are happily
Plowing
A garden

We Came Around

It took a while to unlearn men
And wile away
The gluey dew
We bloomed as children

One click
Innocence

Inquisitive but not naive
The spirit without the meat

We came around again
(We never meant to leave)

It was almost too late
Poisoned by another's hate

Click again for insolence
(This is not the way)

Click three times
There's nothing left to say

Run amok and play
Eat the day

Tenets of Abuse

Unconditional love is a form of conditioning.

Unconditional love
 is a form
  of conditioning

Bull whip
        Crack snap
Love the symbol
        and the pact

Twist the hammer
        Strike the vice
Crush yourself
        To their device

Suffering is not proof of love.

  Suffering
        is not
                proof of love

Break the pattern
Dropkick Saturn
Mythology
        is not
Biology

Run
Reshape
Become
Escape

Lizard Brain

That lyric
About no longer feeding
The backyard-living lizard

Hits different

When the dirt patch
        Is my amygdala's
Brain snatch

I just wanted someone to be
        nice to me
No conditions
Expectations at nil

It was just a handshake
        Until mistaken
Then it was an atom bomb
        wrapped in bacon

Now there's a
        dead pig
Feeding Magdala

And she keeps taking charge

I just wanted to be polite
        Instead I'm trapped
In Fight or Flight

It's Falling

I read my name in the rain
    It's falling

Hits the ground
    in a puddle dance

Unleaded iridescence
    Makes a party of my puddle

Swirl and prance
The world's last chance
    Is Past

Sometimes It's Hard
to Know the Difference Between
Starting Up a New Business
and Entering a Life of Crime

Contracts curl heads around
what could have been highs

Happy to do some work
Eager to receive on time

(Where did it come from?)

No harm done
A little supply chain
        sabotage
Robin Hooding it
        never felt so good

Take words from
        the Jet Stream
                of unconsciousness
Wend and Wind them
        Consciously
                Into understanding
Without comprehension

Marketing as a way of life
        Are you kenning it?

Saturate
        the market share

Repeat transaction
        Repeat

Rabid racer
Money pacer
Untuck luck
and Don't Bother
to give a buck

Agile waterfall
Tripping down rocks

Debilitating
        pleasure
Increasing
        pressure

(They're killing us)

Grandma Banyan

The air changes
      beneath your beaming
        branches
Under cover of twinkling
      light
Raining through your
      leaves

Your embrace is
      soundless
A round caress
      smoothing out
        my gentle mess

Rest in yourself
As I reset myself
      in you

Balmy and calm
Swaying

There's no reaching
No strife of life

A mind at rest
      Straying
Memory of
      Staying
Silently
      Laying

in a nook of you

Canopy arches from ground
        to sky
        to never be found

Earth below gave you up
Roots on high

I swallow the image of you
        Upright and bold
The largest tree
        With the smallest hold

I Break My Back

1.
Deep thock
     Like a punch to the lungs
Can't talk
     Life is now broken rungs

I stand up straight
There's too much weight

Caving in my chest for years
Like a toy with wound-down gears

Backpack on a broken stack
Each breath is me on the rack

2.
One quick twist
Bone to Grist

Clock tock
     What was is gone
Self-mock
     Pain is a yawn

I rest and wait
Relax my gait

There's no ladder to climb
This is not the before
I can make my own door

Future (Im)Perfect

A clattering of Bones
      Approaches

Hold my breath
Don't move a step
Maybe it will miss me

Shamble racket
of creaking clank-bits
Banging rancor that seethes clangor

Wait
      That's wrong

Feel sight through sound
      Without turning round

It's click-clack pattering
      Not bone-battering

That clattering
It's dusty and old
Hooves clopping on stone
Cane-bapping, toe-tapping

Breathe full
And face the Bones
Embrace the gait of aging

When Memory Fails

A hundred thousand
fluttering wings drop from the air
but don't land

Tasmanian devils whorl through an infinite
loop of extinction and
yelping feigned existence that looks
like the location of keys but is
simply the last place
love fell

Caustic tremors shatter
lines and figures
once clear
precise and sensible
Beautiful mathematics
a scatter and shimmer
and cutting
what they used to support and
shine

Moss flowers digest the
remnants of the remaining
ramparts of
that word that
thing that what's that that

Why am I in the kitchen

Glitter Pitch

It's always 30 years ago with you
          except back when it was only 10
or that 1 time when we clawed
          a piece out of Now

We put it in a human cage
          fed it our rage

Calmer people lie about the Moment
Serene, placid; they're submissive to it
Their Now is 1 shining piece of glitter
          breezing by at the edge
          of a picture of possibility

Our Now
          glimpsed the shucking wall
It roiled away at our frivolous bits
          met us, rale for rale
Every voice returned undone
          A dark-sparkling sun

We wove ourselves together
          separately
Golden shards of our reconstructions
          poised at each others' backs
Reflecting the blinding glitter-pitch
          of Now

But that was 30 years ago
          or 10
In the newness of the Now
          there is no Then

Apocalypsing

Ribbons of light
        Stream through us
Razors of Life
        Searing
Healing as quick as they cut

Suffering oneness
        Clasp hands and scream out darkness

Teeming downward river
        Eviscerates memory bodily
Slices as they unfold

We break thought and movement
        Pass each pinprick sword-flick of being

Eccentric abrasion holds us
        Breath to flesh

We end time

Dream Stars

The sparkle in the dark
Called me hard and low
To grasp a star and seed it

They burn
      you know
Dreams burn when you catch them
So remember to let go

They aren't perfection
And need room
      like us
To grow

The Necessity of Distance

We spelled out our nuances
Reaching above the baseness of existence
      (Not for each other
      It was selfishness)
Forcing Beauty out of squalor
Like milk from a dung-covered cow

I didn't notice the Deep Freeze
Until I wandered off distracted
It was the second time
I left our loose and wily congress

      (It was a slow drop
      A melting drip of leaving)

It was a motley band I left
      My voice echoes
      So many absences
      Of different distances

I didn't want you to follow
      Except when I really did
The bulk of you
      (in plural)
Were ice-packed to the spot

The exception to our lack of rule
Was a special conglomeration
      (more like a pack)
Who faced away unburdened

In our various times of night

We may set up a howl
To find each other stumbled
          or humbled
Or proud

The space between
          Us
Allows for our reach to proceed

It was just a Dream

You ate my heart
        in a dream
Rabid
Insatiable

You untied my ribcage
        Gently insinuated my ribs apart
Whispered song tongues to my ears
And slipped a slender hand inside

You squeezed with each contraction
Adding tightness til I screamed

You wrenched it
But it would not come
Yank, pull, throttle

The teeth of your havoc
        tore in

Awake someday
I smelted my ribcage closed
I don't need to
        bend

About the Author

You're getting this in first person whether you
agree with it as reasonable artistic choice or not.

I'm Sarah Soward, and I write poetry again.
Finally.

Poems used to flow out of me in a torrent. One
day, they stopped. I don't remember why.

Somewhere in the middle of then and now,
I put away that part of my mind and wrote
innumerable instructional documents, art books,
and co-authored a tech book.

Bits and bobs of my earlier poetry are scattered across
the country like chickens in an alligator ranch. I'll
decide later if those existing chickens will be saved
from the alligators or left to cluck out my words where
they landed. In the meantime, more collections of new
poetry will happen.

My natural tendencies lean toward chaos
and wandering off. (Perhaps that should be a
warning in the forward?) I do tend to finish
things, though. Point being, the threads of each
collection whisper when they don't shout. If
everything were obvious this wouldn't be fun.

It feels wrong to have all this prose in a poetry
book.

Goodbye.

Related works by the author

Rhinotopia, Beginnings
Self-Portraits of the Apocalypse

More ways to find my work

sarahsoward.com
instagram.com/sarahsoward
facebook.com/sarahsoward
I pop onto various other social media platforms too.

The cover artwork is a detail image from
Sarah Soward's painting, *Monoceros Nyx.*

www.ingramcontent.com/pod-product-compliance
Lightning Source LLC
Chambersburg PA
CBHW021812150726
47989CB00004B/1897